IF I MET AN ICE AGE ANIMAL

IF I PLAYED RING TOSS WITH A WOOLLY RHINOCEROS

by Jenna Lee Gleisner
illustrated by Michelle Simpson

GRASSHOPPER

Tools for Parents & Teachers

Grasshopper Books enhance imagination and introduce the earliest readers to fiction with fun storylines and illustrations. The easy-to-read text supports early reading experiences with repetitive sentence patterns and sight words.

Before Reading

- Discuss the cover illustration. What do readers see?
- Look at the picture glossary together. Discuss the words.

Read the Book

- Read the book to the child, or have him or her read independently.
- "Walk" through the book and look at the illustrations. Who is the main character? What is happening in the story?

After Reading

- Prompt the child to think more. Ask: The main character imagines playing ring toss with a woolly rhinoceros. If you could play a game with any animal, what game and animal would you choose? Why?

Grasshopper Books are published by Jump!
5357 Penn Avenue South
Minneapolis, MN 55419
www.jumplibrary.com

Library of Congress Cataloging-in-Publication Data

Names: Gleisner, Jenna Lee, author.
Simpson, Michelle (Illustrator), illustrator.
Title: If I played ring toss with a woolly rhinoceros
by Jenna Lee Gleisner; illustrated by Michelle Simpson.
Description: Minneapolis, MN: Jump!, Inc., 2023.
Series: If I met an Ice Age animal | Includes index.
Audience: Ages 5-8.
Identifiers: LCCN 2021060814 (print)
LCCN 2021060815 (ebook)
ISBN 9781636909486 (hardcover)
ISBN 9781636909493 (paperback)
ISBN 9781636909509 (ebook)
Subjects: CYAC: Woolly rhinoceros–Fiction.
Rhinoceroses–Fiction. | Prehistoric animals–Fiction.
LCGFT: Picture books.
Classification: LCC PZ7.1.G5885 Ifj 2023 (print)
LCC PZ7.1.G5885 (ebook)
DDC [E]–dc23
LC record available at https://lccn.loc.gov/2021060814
LC ebook record available at https://lccn.loc.gov/2021060815

Editor: Eliza Leahy
Direction and Layout: Anna Peterson
Illustrator: Michelle Simpson

Printed in the United States of America at
Corporate Graphics in North Mankato, Minnesota.

Table of Contents

Horns and Rings

Today is the school fair. My favorite game is ring toss. I got the ring around the woolly rhinoceros's horn!

What if I played ring toss with a real woolly rhinoceros? I wonder.

If I played ring toss with a woolly rhino, I'd have to go back to the Ice Age. Woolly rhinos have been extinct for more than 10,000 years!

Everything is covered in ice and snow. I'd have to dress warm. But the woolly rhino has thick, shaggy hair. She is built for the cold.

I try to get the rings around the rhino's two horns. But she is tall. Her front horn is *even* taller!

She sweeps away snow with
her horns. She looks for food.
Woolly rhinos were herbivores.

When she stops to graze, I toss a ring.
Extra points for the tall horn!

If I played ring toss with a woolly rhino, her calf would want to play, too. Its horns are shorter. This is tricky!

In the distance, two males fight for the female's attention.

They come over. They want to play, too!

Just then, we hear something. A saber-toothed cat is coming our way!

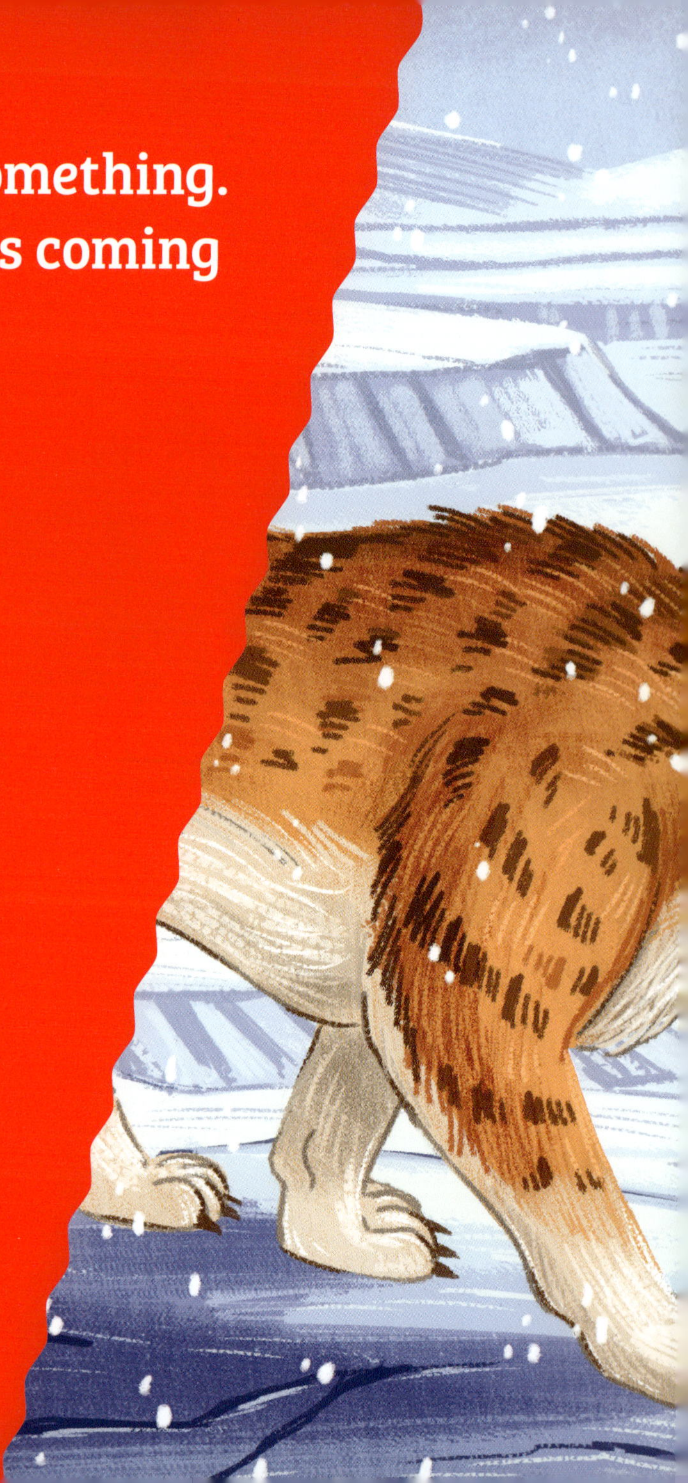

The mom fights the cat.
She uses her horns.
She protects her calf.
She protects me, too.

Phew! We are safe.

"Thanks for playing," I say. "But I think I'll stick to normal ring toss."

Parts of a Woolly Rhinoceros

Woolly rhinoceroses were about 12 feet (3.6 meters) long and six feet (1.8 m) tall. They weighed up to 6,000 pounds (2,720 kilograms). Take a look at the parts of a woolly rhinoceros.

Picture Glossary

calf
A young woolly rhinoceros.

extinct
No longer found alive and known about only through fossils or history.

graze
To feed on grass and other plants that grow close to the ground.

herbivores
Animals that eat plants.

Ice Age
A period of time, about 10,000 years ago, when a large part of Earth was covered with ice.

sweeps
Clears away.

Index

To Learn More

FACT SURFER

Finding more information is as easy as 1, 2, 3.

1. Go to www.factsurfer.com
2. Enter "**ifIplayedringtosswithawoollyrhinoceros**" into the search box.
3. Choose your book to see a list of websites.